U.S. PRESIDENTIAL ELECTIONS: HOW THEY WORK

FUND-RAISING FOR PRESIDENTIAL CANDIDATES

BARBARA MARTINA LINDE

PowerKiDS press
New York

Published in 2020 by The Rosen Publishing Group, Inc.
29 East 21st Street, New York, NY 10010

Copyright © 2020 by The Rosen Publishing Group, Inc.

All rights reserved. No part of this book may be reproduced in any form without permission in writing from the publisher, except by a reviewer.

First Edition

Editor: Rachel Gintner
Book Design: Tanya Dellaccio
Acknowledgement: Michael Roy, research assistant

Photo Credits: Cover MANDEL NGAN/AFP/Getty Images; p. 5 (both) Gary Knapp/Getty Images News/Getty Images; pp. 7, 29 Brooks Kraft/Corbis News/Getty Images; p. 8 (Andrew Jackson) https://upload.wikimedia.org/wikipedia/commons/d/d1/Andrew_jackson_headFXD.jpg; p. 9 (George H.W. Bush) Ira Wyman/Sygma/Getty Images; p. 11 CHRIS DELMAS/AFP/Getty Images; p. 13 Ethan Miller/Getty Images News/Getty Images; p. 14 https://upload.wikimedia.org/wikipedia/commons/4/42/FDR_1944_Color_Portrait.jpg; p. 15 Joe Raedle/Getty Images News/Getty Images; pp. 16, 17, 24, 25 PAUL J. RICHARDS/AFP/Getty Images; p. 19 (top) Chip Somodevilla/Getty Images News/Getty Images; p. 19 (bottom) Mark Van Scyoc/Shutterstock.com; p. 21 (top) https://upload.wikimedia.org/wikipedia/commons/e/ec/Richard_Nixon_presidential_portrait.jpg; p. 21 (bottom) REDPIXEL PL/Shutterstock.com; p. 23 Anthony Jacobs/Getty Images News/Getty Images; p. 27 (top) LUKE FrAZZA/AFP/Getty Images; p. 27 (bottom) https://upload.wikimedia.org/wikipedia/commons/d/d2/%22Profile_in_Courage%22_award.JPG.

Cataloging-in-Publication Data

Names: Linde, Barbara Martina.
Title: Fundraising for presidential candidates / Barbara Martina Linde.
Description: New York : PowerKids Press, 2020. | Series: U.S. presidential elections: how they work | Includes glossary and index.
Identifiers: ISBN 9781725310780 (pbk.) | ISBN 9781725310803 (library bound) | ISBN 9781725310797 (6 pack)
Subjects: LCSH: Campaign funds–United States–Juvenile literature. | Political campaigns–United States–Juvenile literature. | Money–Political aspects–United States–Juvenile literature.
Classification: LCC JK1991.L563 2020 | DDC 324.7'80973–dc23

Manufactured in the United States of America

CPSIA Compliance Information: Batch # CWPK20. For Further Information contact Rosen Publishing, New York, New York at 1-800-237-9932.

CONTENTS

HOW TO BECOME PRESIDENT 4
WHY CANDIDATES NEED MONEY 6
WHY PEOPLE SUPPORT CANDIDATES 8
WHO DONATES? 10
HOW DO CANDIDATES RAISE FUNDS? 12
POLITICAL ACTION COMMITTEES (PACS) . . . 14
SUPER PACS 16
THE FEDERAL ELECTIONS
    COMMISSION (FEC) 18
PUBLIC FUNDING 20
THE FUTURE OF PUBLIC FUNDING 22
HARD AND SOFT MONEY 24
THE BIPARTISAN CAMPAIGN
    REFORM ACT (BCRA) 26
THE CITIZENS UNITED CASE 28
FOR THE FUTURE 30
GLOSSARY 31
INDEX 32
WEBSITES 32

HOW TO BECOME PRESIDENT

Every four years, Americans vote for president of the United States. More than 230 million Americans are legally allowed to vote. In recent years, about 138 million people actually do so. A candidate must win as many of those votes as he or she can. Since 2004, every winner has received more than 60 million votes. But how can a candidate get those votes?

Running a campaign is very expensive. Candidates must spend huge amounts of money. Some candidates are wealthy. They spend a lot of their own money. However, even rich candidates often don't have enough of their own money. They need to raise funds. They go out and get money from voters. Let's find out how presidential candidates raise funds for their **campaigns**!

PATH TO THE PRESIDENCY

BETWEEN 1980 AND 2012, THE TOTAL AMOUNT OF MONEY SPENT IN PRESIDENTIAL ELECTIONS INCREASED FROM $225 MILLION TO NEARLY $3 BILLION!

Before he became president, Barack Obama spent many long hours and days talking to voters all over the country.

WHY CANDIDATES NEED MONEY

Candidates have to let voters get to know them. Since they can't talk to everyone in person, they use the media. They pay for television and radio commercials. They buy ads in newspapers and magazines and run websites. Candidates visit many states. They may fly, or have special cars or buses. They pay for hotels, food, and meeting rooms. They may also pay experts to help them plan their campaigns.

Candidates rent office space in many places. They pay staff members to work in these offices. The offices need supplies such as computers, pens, paper, stamps, and telephones. Campaigns often rent large rooms to hold fund-raising events. Candidates hope to bring in more money than they spend; these activities are to raise money, not necessarily to connect with voters.

PATH TO THE PRESIDENCY
THE MOST EXPENSIVE PRESIDENTIAL CAMPAIGN SO FAR WAS BETWEEN BARACK OBAMA AND JOHN MCCAIN. THEY SPENT A TOTAL OF OVER $1 BILLION.

Presidential candidates rely on campaign staff and volunteers to make their campaign successful. Staff and supllies cost money, and that investment keeps these offices running.

WHY PEOPLE SUPPORT CANDIDATES

Most people want a candidate who will be a good leader. Many people have ideas about how to best run the country. There may be laws they don't like. There may also be laws they want to have made. Therefore, the public listens to the candidates. Then they choose the one with ideas similar to theirs. They think this person will be a good leader. They **donate** money to this candidate. Other people simply vote based on who they don't want to win!

THE SPOILS SYSTEM

PRESIDENT ANDREW JACKSON WAS ELECTED IN 1828. HE IS KNOWN FOR CREATING THE "SPOILS SYSTEM." AFTER HE WAS ELECTED, HE FIRED NEARLY ONE THOUSAND GOVERNMENT WORKERS. HE GAVE THEIR JOBS TO HIS POLITICAL SUPPORTERS. JACKSON THOUGHT THIS WAS A WAY TO REDUCE **CORRUPTION** AND LAZINESS AMONG GOVERNMENT WORKERS. HE CLAIMED HE WAS BRINGING IN PEOPLE TO HELP HIM. MANY OTHERS SAID HIS ACTIONS WERE CORRUPT.

President George H. W. Bush spoke at many campaign rallies. He was elected as president in 1988.

Sometimes people or groups make large donations. They may hope that they can affect a candidate's policies. Some people may hope the president they helped elect will appoint them to a government job. Companies may expect a president to make or change laws to help their businesses.

WHO DONATES?

As of 2018, citizens can legally donate up to $2,800 to each candidate. Youth who are under age 18 can donate. But, they have to use their own money. An adult can't give them money to donate. **Green card** holders may donate. Candidates can donate as much as they like to their own campaigns. Churches, however, can't donate. A **foreign national** can't donate at all. Foreign governments can't donate, either.

Businesses can give money. So can labor unions and trade groups. Political parties can donate to candidates, too.

Supporters can donate their time, as well. A person might volunteer to work in a campaign office. They might perform other services, such as registering voters or driving people to the polls on Election Day.

Presidential candidates make it easy for their supporters to donate money.

HOW DO CANDIDATES RAISE FUNDS?

A fundraiser can be a large or a small event. It can be a fancy dinner in a restaurant, or supporters can have an afternoon picnic in the park. Fund-raising parties also occur. If the group is small, **donors** have more time to talk to the candidate. People pay to go to these events. The amount may be as low as $25. Or, it could be thousands of dollars!

Some candidates send out letters, texts, or emails. They explain their ideas and ask for money. Volunteers run phone banks to call people and ask for money. Candidates often give T-shirts, yard signs, and other things to donors. Nowadays, social media is a popular way to raise funds. Candidates create websites that take credit cards.

PATH TO THE PRESIDENCY

CROWDFUNDING FOR OFFICE IS ONE OF THE NEWEST AND LEAST EXPENSIVE WAYS TO RAISE FUNDS. A CANDIDATE SETS UP AN ONLINE CROWDFUNDING PAGE. VIEWERS LOOK AT PICTURES AND VIDEOS THAT TELL ABOUT THE CANDIDATE. PEOPLE CAN DONATE ONCE, OR THEY CAN SIGN UP TO GIVE MONEY EVERY MONTH.

Volunteers at phone banks call voters. They explain the candidate's ideas and ask for money.

POLITICAL ACTION COMMITTEES (PACS)

Companies, unions, and membership groups can't give money directly to a candidate. But, they can give money through a political action committee. A PAC is a private group. A corporation can have a PAC. A labor union or a membership group can have a PAC as well. Only members of the group can give to the PAC. A candidate can set up his or her own PAC, too. A political party or a candidate can't run a PAC.

PATH TO THE PRESIDENCY

THE FIRST PAC WAS CREATED IN 1944. IT RAISED MONEY FOR PRESIDENT FRANKLIN D. ROOSEVELT'S REELECTION. THE LAW SAID CAMPAIGN MONEY COULD NOT COME FROM WORKER'S UNION DUES, OR FEES. SO, THE PAC ASKED UNION WORKERS TO DONATE MONEY. THIS WAS LEGAL.

PACs often pay for billboards, commercials, and other advertising opportunities to share their views on issues and candidates.

PACs can **bundle** donations. One person collects money from others. That person then gives it to the campaign. Each PAC has a single focus. It might be helping farmers. Or, it might be improving voting rights. PACs must work under many rules. Still, they can plan directly with candidates.

SUPER PACS

A Super PAC is also a private group. It can raise as much money as it wants. Businesses, labor unions, and membership groups often form super PACs. Like PACs, super PACs also bundle donations. Super PACs, though, do not have to focus on any one issue. There's no limit to their spending amount. But, there are many rules for spending their

In 2013, the Ready for Hillary super PAC mailed 50,000 bumper stickers to potential donors to seek support for possible presidential candidate Hillary Clinton during the 2016 presidential election.

money. They can't give money directly to a candidate or party. Super PACs may not speak with candidates. They can't plan with candidates about how to use their money.

Suppose a super PAC likes one candidate. The super PAC can run ads against the other one. It can send out flyers and emails. In this way, super PACs help their candidates win.

THE FEDERAL ELECTIONS COMMISSION (FEC)

The **Federal** Elections Commission, or FEC, is an independent government **agency**. That means the **executive branch** can't control its work. The FEC watches over campaign finances. Before the 1970s, there were some laws and rules about campaign finance. But, candidates didn't always obey them. Some information was kept secret. The public didn't know what was going on. Congress created the FEC to change this. It started its work in 1975.

The FEC has three main jobs. The first is getting and keeping records on campaign fund-raising and spending. Next, the FEC makes sure that everyone keeps to the legal spending and donating limits. Last, the FEC manages public funding for presidential campaigns. The public can look up information on the FEC website.

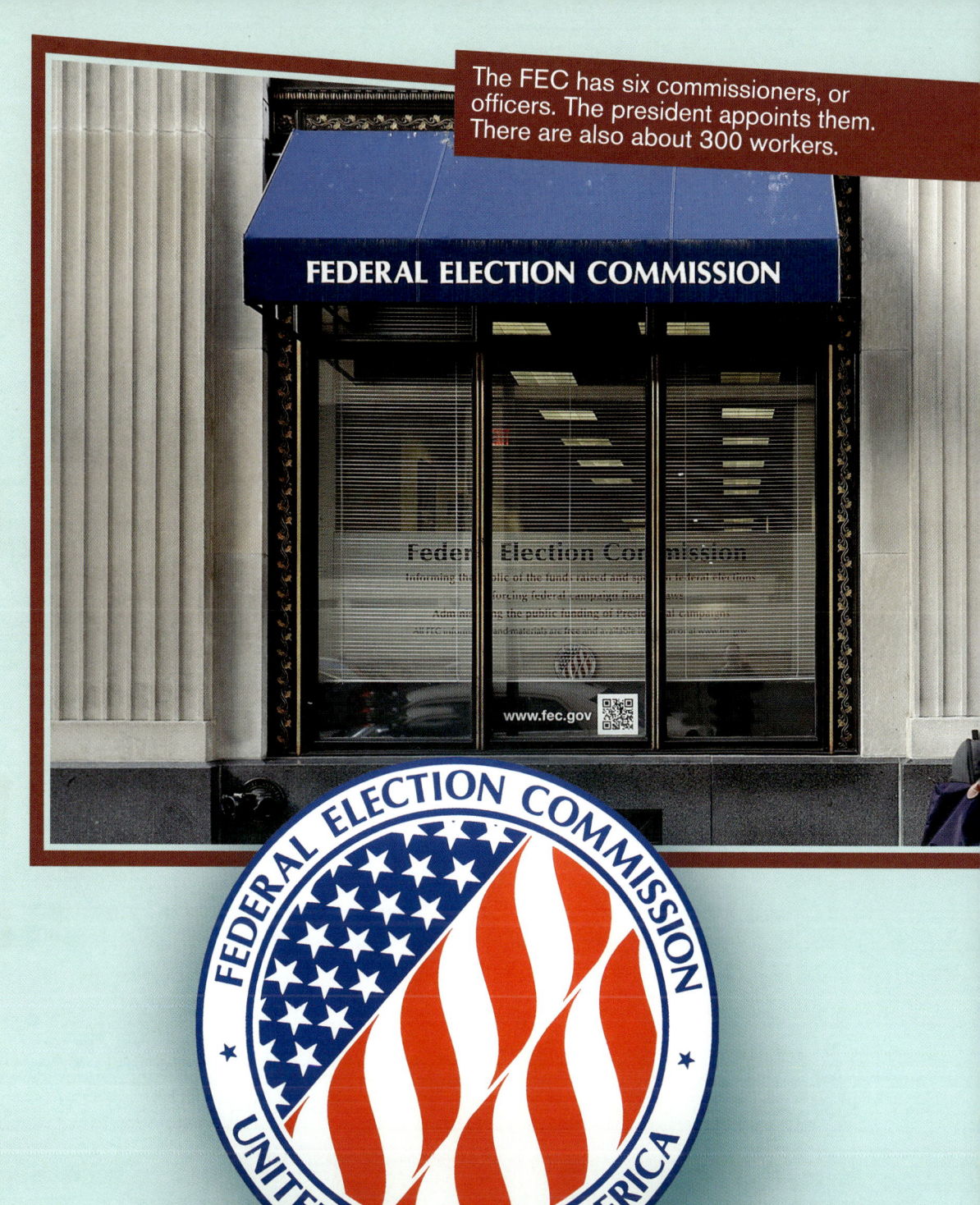

The FEC has six commissioners, or officers. The president appoints them. There are also about 300 workers.

PUBLIC FUNDING

Congress also started a system of public funding. It was meant to be a fair way to give presidential candidates money. The FEC would make sure that the candidates had enough money. Then they would not be tempted to accept other large donations. These might lead to corruption.

Public funding for presidential campaigns comes from federal tax money. When people file their income taxes, they can give three dollars to the Presidential Election Campaign Fund. The FEC knows the total amount of money in the fund. It gives the money to the candidates. Candidates have to agree to spend only the public money. They can spend up to $50,000 of their own money. But, they can't take any other contributions.

The federal tax form has a box to check to make a donation.

QUID PRO QUO

IN 1971, REPRESENTATIVES OF THE DAIRY INDUSTRY MADE A PLAN. THEY WOULD GIVE $2 MILLION TO PRESIDENT NIXON'S ELECTION CAMPAIGN. IN RETURN, NIXON WOULD GIVE THEM $100 MILLION TO HELP THEIR BUSINESSES. THIS DEAL WAS CALLED A QUID PRO QUO. IT MEANS "A FAVOR FOR A FAVOR" AND IS A FORM OF CORRUPTION. PEOPLE FOUND OUT ABOUT THIS BAD DEAL. IT WAS PART OF THE REASON THAT NIXON LEFT OFFICE. THE GOVERNMENT MADE STRONGER CAMPAIGN FINANCE LAWS AFTER THAT.

THE FUTURE OF PUBLIC FUNDING

In 1976, each candidate got $21.8 million. The amount grew for each election. By 2008, each person got $84.1 million. Then something different happened. Barack Obama became the first candidate not to accept public funding. He said that his opponent, John McCain, had a lot of money from other sources. Obama thought the public money was not enough to beat McCain. In the end, neither candidate took the public funding. Obama raised about $730 million. McCain raised about $333 million.

In 2016, the public funding amount for each candidate was $96.1 million. The Democratic nominee was Hillary Clinton. She did not take the public financing. Neither did Republican Donald Trump. Some experts think that candidates will no longer take public funding, but others disagree.

Campaign spending by Barack Obama and John McCain in 2008 marked a trend, a change from using public funding to using private resources.

HARD AND SOFT MONEY

The terms "hard" and "soft" money don't mean metal coins and paper bills! Hard money means donations to the candidate. The FEC controls the spending. Soft money goes to a political party. It does not need to stay within FEC limits. This money can be spent for party building and other items. It's not in direct support of, or against, any candidate.

Suppose a candidate takes a donation from a person or group. He or she uses it to make a TV commercial. That's hard money.

Suppose someone makes a TV ad. The ad is about an issue that is important to a candidate. The person is spending soft money. He or she produces the ad and pays to air it.

Buying T-shirts, magnets, stickers, and other items from a candidate's campaign is one way of financially supporting them.

THE BIPARTISAN CAMPAIGN REFORM ACT (BCRA)

The **Bipartisan** Campaign Reform Act became law in 2002. Senators John McCain and Russ Feingold wrote it. The men wanted both parties to work together.

The law dealt with fund-raising and spending for federal elections. It said national parties could not ask for, or use, soft money. State parties couldn't use soft money for federal elections. Federal candidates could no longer use soft money for their elections. The law also made changes to issue **advocacy**. These are ads that tell voters about a topic. But, the ads don't directly say how to vote. Ads about gun control and climate change are examples. Corporations and labor unions could no longer pay for these ads. The ads could not be shown within 60 days of an election.

The BCRA is also known as the McCain-Feingold Act for the senators who sponsored it. John McCain was a Republican senator from Arizona. Russ Feingold was a Democratic senator from Wisconsin.

PATH TO THE PRESIDENCY

IN 1999, THE TWO SENATORS WON THE JOHN F. KENNEDY PROFILE IN COURAGE AWARD FOR THEIR WORK ON CAMPAIGN FINANCE REFORM.

THE CITIZENS UNITED CASE

A big change in campaign finance came in 2010. The **Supreme Court** heard the case of *Citizens United v. Federal Election Commission*. Citizens United is a corporation. It had made a video about Hillary Clinton's career in politics. It was not in favor of Hillary as a candidate. Under the BCRA, the video could not be shown because it came out so close to the 2008 **primary election**. Citizens United appealed this decision. They said their right to free speech was being limited. The Supreme Court agreed. They struck down some of the BCRA's rules.

As a result, businesses, labor unions, and other groups could spend as much money as they wanted. But, they still could not plan or work directly with the candidates.

PATH TO THE PRESIDENCY

IN 2016, SPENDING BY THE PRESIDENTIAL CANDIDATES THEMSELVES ADDED UP TO LESS THAN HALF OF THE TOTAL AMOUNT SPENT ON FUND-RAISING.

Justices Roberts, Kennedy, Scalia, Alito, and Thomas agreed with Citizens United. Justices Stevens, Ginsburg, Breyer, and Sotomayor disagreed.

FOR THE FUTURE

Fund-raising is an important part of every presidential campaign. Without funds, the candidates can't get out their messages. Candidates need to know the laws about fund-raising. That way, they can run honest campaigns.

Voters need to hear from candidates so they can make educated decisions about their votes. It's important for donors to understand how and where their money goes. They have the right to expect that their money is being used lawfully. Lawmakers think about the needs of the candidates and the rights of voters. Their goal should be to make fair campaign finance laws.

During the next presidential campaign, pay attention. Look at how the candidates are raising funds. See if you can figure out if they're obeying fund-raising laws.

GLOSSARY

advocacy: Supporting a person or an idea.

agency: A department of the government.

bipartisan: Involving two political parties.

bundle: To combine or group together.

campaign: Activities and events to win a political election.

corruption: Actions that are not honest or are against the law.

donate: To give money, time, or things to help a person or a group.

donor: A person or group that gives money, time, or things.

executive branch: The president, vice president, and members of the cabinet.

federal: Having to do with the central government.

foreign national: Someone who is not a citizen of the United States and has not been legally permitted to live in the United States.

green card: A document from the government saying the person is legally allowed to live in the United States.

primary election: An election to choose a candidate for a presidential election.

supreme court: The highest court in either a nation or state.

INDEX

B
BIPARTISAN CAMPAIGN REFORM ACT (BCRA), 26, 28
BUSINESSES, 10

C
CITIZENS UNITED, 28
CROWDFUNDING, 12

E
ELECTION DAY, 10

F
FEDERAL ELECTIONS COMMISSION (FEC), 18, 20
FOREIGN GOVERNMENTS, 10

H
HARD MONEY, 24, 25

J
JACKSON, ANDREW, 8

P
POLITICAL ACTION COMMITTEES (PACS), 14
POLITICAL PARTIES, 10
PRESIDENTIAL ELECTION CAMPAIGN FUND, 20
PUBLIC FUNDING, 20, 22

R
ROOSEVELT, FRANKLIN D., 14

S
SOFT MONEY, 24, 25
SUPER PACS, 16, 17
SUPREME COURT, 28

WEBSITES

Due to the changing nature of Internet links, PowerKids Press has developed an online list of websites related to the subject of this book. This site is updated regularly. Please use this link to access the list: www.powerkidslinks.com/uspe/funding